W9-AYH-479

Isaac Asimov's
21st Century
Library of the
Universe

Past and Present

Astronomy in Ancient Times

BY ISAAC ASIMOV

WITH REVISIONS AND UPDATING BY RICHARD HANTULA

Gareth Stevens Publishing
A WORLD ALMANAC EDUCATION GROUP COMPANY

Please visit our web site at: www.garethstevens.com
For a free color catalog describing Gareth Stevens Publishing's list of high-quality
books and multimedia programs, call 1-800-542-2595 (USA) or 1-800-387-3178 (Canada).
Gareth Stevens Publishing's fax: (414) 332-3567.

Library of Congress Cataloging-in-Publication Data available upon request from publisher.
Fax (414) 336-0157 for the attention of the Publishing Records Department.

ISBN 0-8368-3978-1 (lib. bdg.)

This edition first published in 2006 by
Gareth Stevens Publishing
A Member of the WRC Media Family of Companies
330 West Olive Street, Suite 100
Milwaukee, WI 53212 USA

Revised and updated edition © 2006 by Gareth Stevens, Inc. Original edition published in 1988 by
Gareth Stevens, Inc. under the title *Ancient Astronomy*. Second edition published in 1995 by
Gareth Stevens, Inc. under the title *Astronomy in Ancient Times*. Text © 2006 by Nightfall, Inc.
End matter and revisions © 2006 by Gareth Stevens, Inc.

Series editor: Mark J. Sachner
Art direction: Tammy West
Cover design: Melissa Valuch
Layout adaptation: Melissa Valuch and Jenni Gaylord
Picture research: Kathy Keller
Additional picture research: Diane Laska-Swanke
Artwork commissioning: Kathy Keller and Laurie Shock
Production director: Jessica Morris
Production coordinator: Robert Kraus

The editors at Gareth Stevens Publishing have selected science author Richard Hantula to bring
this classic series of young people's information books up to date. Richard Hantula has written
and edited books and articles on science and technology for more than two decades. He was
the senior U.S. editor for the *Macmillan Encyclopedia of Science*.

In addition to Hantula's contribution to this most recent edition, the editors would like to
acknowledge the participation of two noted science authors, Greg Walz-Chojnacki and
Francis Reddy, as contributors to earlier editions of this work.

Printed in the United States of America

1 2 3 4 5 6 7 8 9 09 08 07 06 05

Contents

• Astronomy in Ancient Times •

We live in an enormously large place – the Universe. It's only natural that we would want to understand this place, so scientists and engineers have developed instruments and spacecraft that have told us far more about the Universe than we could possibly imagine.

We have seen planets up close, and spacecraft have even landed on some. We have learned about quasars and pulsars, supernovas and colliding galaxies, and black holes and dark matter. We have gathered amazing data about how the Universe may have come into being and how it may end. Nothing could be more astonishing.

All our knowledge of the Universe started with people who looked at the sky in ancient times and wondered. They did not have scientific instruments. They had only their eyes. Even so, they managed to study the objects in the sky and observe how the objects moved. They even thought about why the movement took place. Our knowledge of the Universe began with these ancient astronomers. We could not have come as far as we have without their early efforts.

A Clear and Pure Sky

In modern times, it is hard to study the night sky. The dust and lights of today's activities hide it. Ancient people had a better, clearer chance to study the sky and see the patterns, or constellations, of the stars.

They drew pictures of constellations that looked like people and animals, and they made up stories to account for the constellations being in the sky. They noticed that the Moon changed its shape from night to night and changed its position against the stars. The earliest calendars, which showed the change of seasons, were probably based on the changes of the Moon. Ancient priests were among the first astronomers. They studied the sky carefully to make sure the calendars were accurate.

Left: Ancient people were fascinated by the rhythms of the sky. They painted on cave walls some of the things they saw there.

Ancient Egypt's Livelihood

The lives of the ancient Egyptians depended on the Nile River. When the river flooded the fields, it brought water and rich soil that made it possible to grow crops.

Egyptian priests carefully recorded when the floods came. The flooding was found to begin every 365 days. So the Egyptians were the first to use a calendar with a 365-day year. Their year began when the bright star Sirius appeared above the eastern horizon at dawn. The priests had noticed that the star rose with the Sun when the flood was due.

The ancient Egyptians also invented sundials to measure the time of day by the movement of the Sun.

Right: Sirius is the brightest star in the sky (not counting the Sun).

Now you see 'em more; now less.

Certain stars, called variable stars, seem to get slightly brighter and then dimmer. Why do they change in brightness? In some cases it's because of processes inside the star. In other cases the star is actually a "binary" system, consisting of a pair of stars, and it dims when one member of the pair eclipses, or blocks, the other. Ancient star watchers might have seen such changes, but did not speak of them. The ancients seemed to believe that the heavens never changed, so maybe they did not want to admit that stars could vary in brightness!

About five thousand years ago, ancient Egyptians used the position of Sirius to predict the annual flooding of the Nile River.

Above: Could this have been an ancient observatory? A story in the Bible tells how the people of a Babylonian city tried to build a stairway to the stars — the Tower of Babel.

Predicting the Future in Babylon

The ancient Babylonians lived two to three thousand or more years ago in what is now Iraq. They were among the very first people worldwide to study the movements of the planets Mercury, Venus, Mars, Jupiter, and Saturn. These planets follow complicated paths among the stars in the sky.

The Babylonians kept detailed records of these paths and learned to predict them. Like many other peoples, they thought that planets' movements gave hints about future happenings on Earth. Modern astrology, which also believes that planets reveal hints about the future, originated with the ancient Babylonians.

Above: In this ancient Babylonian view of the Universe the land rests on a huge ocean, as does the dome of heaven. Babylonia is shown at the center of the land.

Using their knowledge of the sea and sky,
Polynesian sailors safely crossed the vast
Pacific Ocean in fragile boats.

Early Astronomy in China and the Pacific

In ancient China, too, astronomy was important because changes in the sky were thought to mean future dangerous conditions on Earth. The ancient Chinese astronomers watched for any new stars that might appear, as well as eclipses of the Sun and Moon, so they could warn people of future catastrophic events.

Some stars and constellations, like the Big Dipper, always stay in the same part of the sky. This allowed ancient sailors to use the stars to help guide their ships. Observation of the stars was one navigational method used by Polynesians of long ago when they sailed to distant islands over the vast Pacific Ocean.

Right: The compass was invented long ago by the Chinese, who used it not only for finding north and south but also, as in this example, for divination, or fortune-telling.

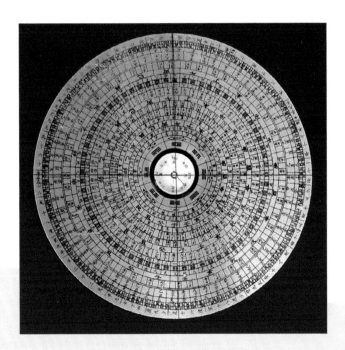

Lesson of the Day

In the 1400s, the Mongol prince Ulugh Beg built an observatory at Samarkand, in what is now Uzbekistan. He also made a star map of 994 stars. It was the best in the world at the time, but its creator was virtually unknown. There were many other unknown ancient astronomers who made great discoveries. For instance, who was the first person to notice Saturn? Who was the first person to determine the coming of the next eclipse? Who was the first person to make an accurate calendar?

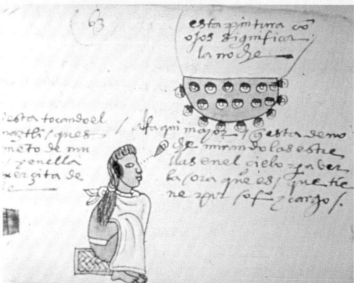

Above: The Caracol, an early observatory located in Chichén Itzá in northern Yucatán, Mexico, was built by the Mayan people about a thousand years ago. The Mayans studied the movement of the planet Venus through openings in the tower's top.

Left: The Aztecs, who built an empire in Mexico after the decline of the Mayans, also watched the sky. They used pictographic writing to record their observations. This old document shows an Aztec astronomer.

Astronomy in the Early Americas

The early Mayans of southern Mexico, Belize, Guatemala, El Salvador, and Honduras developed a complex written language and a clever way of writing numbers. They were the first people in the New World known to keep historical records.

The Mayans observed the movements of the Sun, Moon, and planets – especially Venus. Several of their buildings were designed with the motion of Venus in mind. The building called the Caracol, in Chichén Itzá, was used as an observatory to follow the planet's progress.

The Mayans observed the cycles in which objects in the sky move, and they recorded these cycles in picture books made from tree bark. Fragments of only four of these books survive today, but they, along with inscriptions in stone, show that the Mayans had learned to predict eclipses of the Sun and Moon and the path of Venus. One of the calendars used by the Mayans was even more accurate than the one used by the Spanish when they reached the New World. Most of the books of the great Mayan civilization were destroyed when the Spanish arrived in the early 1500s.

Above: Hundreds of years ago, Anasazi Indians drew a sketch of the Moon and a star on the rocks of New Mexico's Chaco Canyon. Some scientists think the star may represent a star that exploded in a supernova in 1054. The remnants of this supernova in the sky are called the Crab Nebula.

Earth as a Huge Ball

The ancient Greeks made major contributions to astronomy. The earliest Greek astronomers picked up much of their knowledge from the Babylonians. The Greek philosopher Thales predicted an eclipse of the Sun that took place in 585 B.C. He most likely used Babylonian scientific methods to make his prediction.

Around 550 B.C., the Greek philosopher Pythagoras pointed out that the Evening Star and the Morning Star were really the same body. Today, we know that this body is actually the planet Venus. Pythagoras, too, probably made use of Babylonian knowledge.

But Greek astronomy moved beyond the Babylonians. Most people back then thought Earth was flat, but some Greeks thought it might be in the shape of a ball. Some also thought the light of the Moon was really reflected sunlight. Today, we know how right they were!

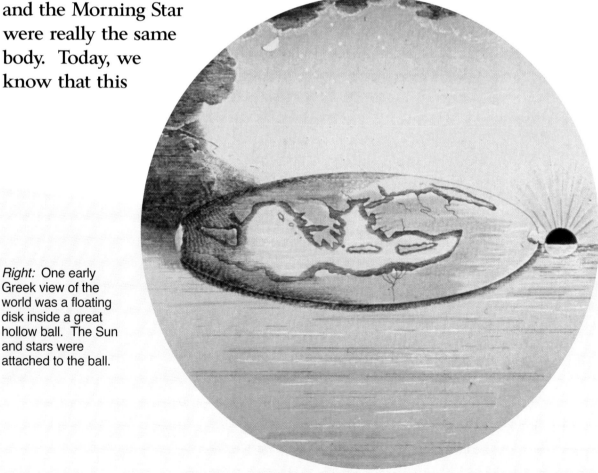

Right: One early Greek view of the world was a floating disk inside a great hollow ball. The Sun and stars were attached to the ball.

The ancient Greek philosopher Pythagoras. He and his followers were skilled in mathematics and astronomy. They were among the first to think of Earth as a huge ball.

15

Celestial Positions

In addition to thinking of Earth as a huge ball, many ancient Greek astronomers believed that it lay at the center of the Universe and that the objects in the sky moved around it in great circles. Each planet moved in a separate circle. According to one common scheme, the Moon was lowest. Then came Mercury, Venus, the Sun, Mars, Jupiter, and Saturn. The stars were farthest out.

Sometimes, however, planets in the sky seem to change directions.

To explain this, the astronomers Hipparchus and Ptolemy developed a detailed system of planetary motions. Ptolemy did his work in about A.D. 150. But he used the work of Hipparchus from about 130 B.C. So it took a long time – about 280 years – and a lot of effort to come up with these ideas about planetary motions. The research was extremely complicated, but it produced important information to help determine the movements of the planets.

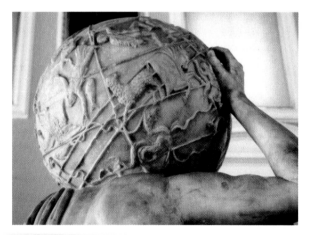

Left: The positions of the constellations shown on this globe – part of an ancient statue in Naples, Italy – are thought by some scientists to be based on a long lost star catalog compiled by the Greek astronomer Hipparchus.

Lost ancient star catalog – found in plain sight?

Hipparchus is believed to have made the first major catalog of stars. The catalog, which was finished in 129 B.C., listed the position and brightness of some 850 stars. The astronomer Ptolemy is said to have used it, but it was later lost. In 2005 an American scientist suggested that a sort of star map based on the lost catalog may have been hiding in plain sight. A famous ancient statue in Naples, Italy, includes a globe that accurately shows the constellations in the positions they had in Hipparchus's time – but not earlier or later. No one had ever before thought to determine precisely what period the globe depicted.

Above: Ptolemy thought the Sun, Moon, and planets circled Earth.

Right: Ptolemy in his observatory. He lived and worked in Alexandria, Egypt.

Early Earthly Statistics

The ancient Greeks tried to find out the size of Earth and of celestial bodies such as the Sun and the Moon. They also attempted to figure out how far these bodies were from Earth. Some of their efforts were surprisingly successful.

One example was the distance around Earth — its circumference — which was found in about 240 B.C. by Eratosthenes, a Greek astronomer who worked in Alexandria, Egypt. Eratosthenes noticed that when the Sun was directly overhead in the city of Syene, it cast a shadow in Alexandria, which was to the north. Based on the angle of the Sun's rays in Alexandria and the distance between the cities, he caculated Earth's circumference at about 25,000 miles (40,000 km).

About a century later, Hipparchus came up with the first relatively accurate figure for the distance to the Moon, He studied Earth's shadow when it eclipsed the Moon. Taking into account the size of the Moon, he decided the distance must be about 240,000 miles (384,000 km).

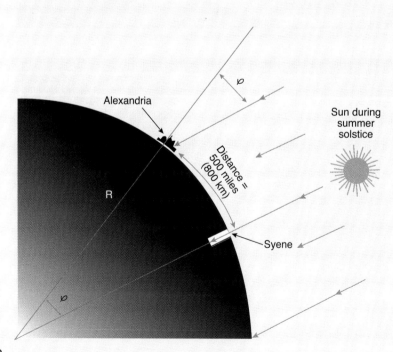

Alexandria

Distance = 500 miles (800 km)

R

Syene

Sun during summer solstice

Left: By combining his observations of the sky with his skill in mathematics, Eratosthenes was able to determine the size of Earth. He noticed that at noon on the first day of summer (the summer solstice), the Sun was directly overhead at Syene, but in Alexandria, which lies north of Syene, its rays came at a angle. Assuming Earth is shaped like a ball, this angle and the distance between the two cities were all the information he needed to calculate the total distance around Earth.

Above: Much of the work of the famous ancient Greek astronomer Ptolemy (pictured) was based on that of Hipparchus, who was born nearly three centuries earlier.

Astronomers in an observatory in Istanbul, Turkey, in the sixteenth century.

American Indians may also have noticed the supernova of 1054. This "supernova bowl" was made by the Mimbres people. It shows a rabbit (a common Moon symbol) near a star surrounded by twenty-three rays. That's the same number of days Chinese astronomers said the supernova could be seen in daylight!

Saved by the Arabs

After Ptolemy, Greek science faded and Europe slowly entered a period known as the Dark Ages. But the Arabs, beginning in the seventh century A.D., set up a large empire, discovered Greek books on science and mathematics, translated them into Arabic, and studied them.

Important advances were made by Arab and other Islamic astronomers. Around 900 A.D., an Arab named Al-Battani, who worked in Syria, introduced new mathematical methods and improved many of Ptolemy's observations.

In about 1150, Europeans began to translate the Arabic versions of the Greek books into Latin. If it hadn't been for the Arabs, Greek science might have been lost!

Right: An Arab astrolabe. Astrolabes – devices used to measure the positions of celestial bodies – were invented by the ancient Greeks and later refined by the Arabs.

Learn some Arabic!

Because of the important role played by the Arabs in the creation of modern astronomy, many of our names for stars come from Arabic. Among them are such major stars as Aldebaran, Altair, Betelgeuse, Deneb, Mira, Rigel, and Vega. Also of Arabic origin are several key words in astronomy, including *zenith* (the point in the sky directly above an observer), *nadir* (the opposite of the zenith), and *azimuth* (an angle distance along the horizon). Another Arabic word is *almanac*, which traditionally referred to a collection of data about astronomy and the weather for a given year.

Copernicus and the Center of the Universe

The ancient Greeks' picture of the Universe — with Earth at the center — was so complicated that scientists looked for a simpler scheme. The Polish astronomer Nicolaus Copernicus thought it would be better to put the Sun at the center, with the planets circling it. This idea had been suggested in the past by a few astronomers, but it never caught on. Earth would have to circle the Sun, too, and this seemed against common sense. But in a book published in 1543, the year he died, Copernicus said his idea would make it much easier to determine planetary positions.

After many decades of argument, most astronomers began to accept his approach. Later, however, they learned that the Sun was not the center of the universe either!

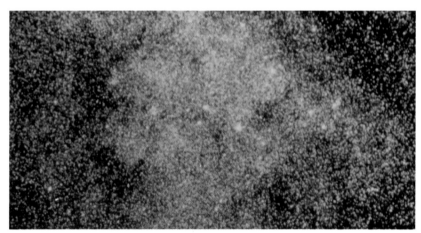

Above: The Gum Nebula, believed by astronomers to be the remains of an ancient supernova.

Supernova — a star as bright as the Moon!

Supernovas are stars that explode in a terrific blaze of light. Sometimes they leave behind a cloud of dust and gas. The Gum Nebula is probably the closest such cloud to Earth. Astronomers think it resulted from the explosion of a star that was about 1,000 light-years from Earth. The explosion may have occurred as many as one million years ago. When it was at its peak, this star must have shone as brightly as the full Moon.

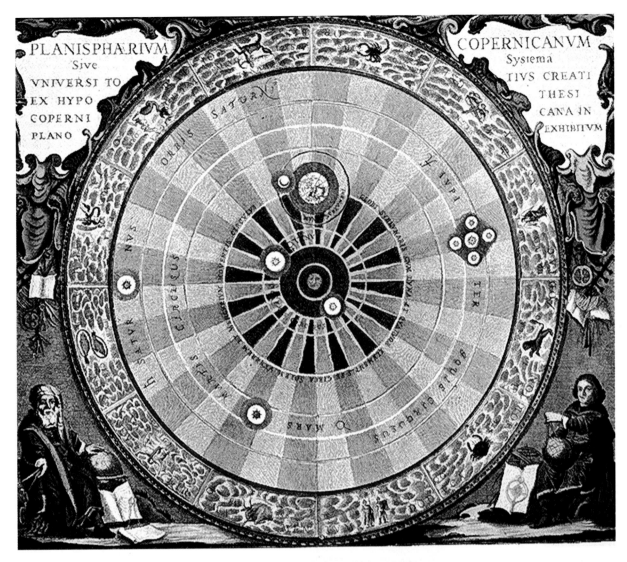

PLANISPHÆRIVM
Sive
VNIVERSI TO
EX HYPO
COPERNI
PLANO

COPERNICANVM
Systema
TIVS CREATI
THESI
CANA IN
EXHIBITIVM

Above: Copernicus's scheme of the universe with the Sun at its center. This view was made by a seventeenth-century map maker who included drawings of Copernicus (*shown in the bottom right corner of the illustration*) and also Aristarchus (*shown bottom left*), an ancient Greek astronomer who suggested that the Sun, not Earth, was the center of the Universe.

Right: A portrait of Copernicus by a seventeenth-century artist.

Tycho Brahe witnessed the explosion of a star in 1572. He recorded the position of this supernova so precisely that modern astronomers have found its remains *(inset)*.

Open to New Viewpoints

A Danish astronomer, Tycho Brahe, had a suspicion that the sky did not always stay the same, as the Greeks had thought. In 1572, he spotted and studied a bright new star in the sky. It eventually faded away. Scientists now know he saw a supernova.

Brahe studied a comet in 1577. He tried to determine its distance from Earth by seeing if it changed its position when viewed from different places. It did not. From this information, Brahe could tell that the comet had to be quite far away, farther than the Moon.

The ancient Greeks had always thought comets were inside our atmosphere. But with updated details about comets from Brahe, scientists became more open to new ideas about the sky.

Left: English astronomer Edmond Halley explained the motions of comets.

Right: Tycho Brahe built this huge instrument, a type of armillary sphere, to measure the positions of the stars and planets.

Comets — ancient enigmas

Early astronomers knew very little about comets. Comets appeared suddenly, moved against the stars unpredictably, and then vanished. People thought they might be special warnings of disaster. It wasn't until 1705 that an English astronomer, Edmond Halley, explained the motions of comets. He showed that they moved around the Sun in unusual, but predictable, orbits. Even so, many people were still frightened by comets.

25

An Astronomical Turning Point

A turning point in astronomy came with the invention of the telescope in Holland in 1608. An Italian astronomer, Galileo Galilei, heard about the new invention and built his own. In 1609, he pointed it toward the heavens for the first time.

Immediately, Galileo discovered many stars that were too dim to see without a telescope. He also found that the Moon was an entire world — with craters, mountains, and what looked like seas. He discovered that the planet Jupiter had moons that moved around it, and that Venus changed shape, just as Earth's Moon did.

This new information didn't fit the Greek views of astronomy, but it did fit the views of Copernicus. At that moment, modern astronomy began!

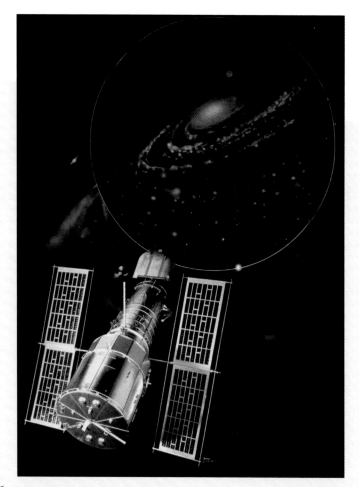

Above: Two of the telescopes used by Galileo (shown here mounted on a special stand in a museum).

Left: Today's astronomers observe the Universe not only with telescopes located on Earth but also with telescopes based in space, such as the Hubble Space Telescope, shown here.

Galileo experiments with his first telescope.

Fact File: Astronomy – Past and Present

The earliest observatories may have been simple open platforms where astronomers could watch the sky with no buildings in the way.

At least five thousand years ago, ancient peoples began arranging large stones in rows or circles that may have been used for religious purposes or perhaps to track the Sun and stars as they moved through the sky. The most famous ancient structure of this kind is a circle of large upright stones called Stonehenge, in England. American Indians also built circles of stones that seem to line up with the Sun and stars and, some scientists think, may have been used to determine when the Sun would rise and when summer would start.

Greek and Arab astronomers used the astrolabe – which means "star-finder" – to sight and predict the movements of the Sun, Moon, planets, and stars, and to tell time.

Before the telescope was invented, perhaps the most advanced observatory of all was the one founded by the Danish astronomer Tycho Brahe in the late 1500s. It used long, open sighting devices to watch the sky.

The telescope was the beginning of modern astronomy. Today, in addition to optical telescopes, which rely on light, astronomers use instruments that pick up other types of electromagnetic radiation from celestial bodies, such as radio waves, X rays, and gamma rays. Such instruments have even been launched into space. Today's instruments make possible discoveries that ancient astronomers never dreamed of.

A brief history of observatories from prehistoric days to the present:

30,000 years ago – Cave drawings by early humans

3000 B.C. – Stonehenge, England

1050 A.D. – Chichén Itzá, Yucatán, Mexico

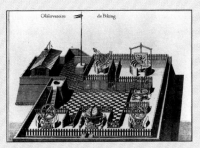

1400s – Beijing Observatory, China

1576 – Tycho Brahe's observatory, Ven, Denmark

1724 – Delhi Observatory, India

1839 – Pulkovo Observatory, St. Petersburg, Russia

1864 – Observatory in Quito, Ecuador

1967 – Mauna Kea Observatory, Hawaii

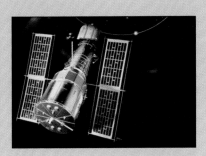

1990 – Hubble Space Telescope

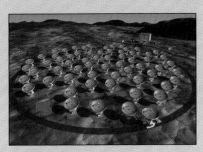

2012 (planned end of construction) – ALMA radio telescope array, Chile

More Books about Astronomy History

Ancient Astronomers. Anthony F. Aveni. (Smithsonian)

The Cambridge Illustrated History of Astronomy. Michael Hoskin, editor (Cambridge University)

Legends, Folklore, and Outer Space. Isaac Asimov (Gareth Stevens)

The Mapping of the Heavens. Peter Whitfield (Pomegranate)

Nicolaus Copernicus: The Earth Is a Planet. Dennis Brindell Fradin and Cynthia Von Buhler (Mondo)

Sky Watchers of Ages Past. Malcolm Weiss (Houghton Mifflin)

The Telescope. Tamra Orr (Franklin Watts)

DVD and Video

The Standard Deviants — Astronomy Adventure. (Cerebellum)

Wonders of the Universe. (York)

Web Sites

The Internet sites listed here can help you learn more about astronomy and its history.

Adler Planetarium & Astronomy Museum.
www.adlerplanetarium.org/history/index.shtml

History for Kids. www.michielb.nl/maya/astro.html

Maya Astronomy Page. www.adlerplanetarium.org/history/index.shtml

Nine Planets. www.seds.org/nineplanets/nineplanets/nineplanets.html

Windows to the Universe. www.windows.ucar.edu/tour/link=/people/people.html

Places to Visit

Here are some museums and centers where you can find a variety of exhibits on astronomy and its history.

Adler Planetarium & Astronomy Museum
1300 S. Lake Shore Drive
Chicago, Illinois 60605-2403

American Museum of Natural History
Rose Center for Earth and Space
Central Park West at 79th Street
New York, NY 10024

Canada Science and Technology Museum
1867 St Laurent Blvd
Ottawa, Ontario K1G 5A3
Canada

Miami Museum of Science & Planetarium
3280 South Miami Avenue
Miami, FL 33129

Museum of Science, Boston
Science Park
Boston, MA 02114

The Science Museum
Exhibition Road
South Kensington
London SW7 2DD
United Kingdom

Glossary

annual: happening once a year.

armillary sphere: an old scientific instrument made of rings that was used to measure the positions of the stars and planets or as a model to show the motions of such celestial bodies.

astrolabe: "star-finder" — a small instrument once used to measure celestial bodies' positions and to tell time.

astrology: the study of the positions of the stars and planets and their supposed influence upon humans and events on Earth.

astronomy: the scientific study of the Universe and the bodies, dust, and gas in it.

atmosphere: the gases that surround a planet, star, or moon. Earth's atmosphere consists of oxygen, nitrogen, carbon dioxide, and other gases.

binary star: a system of two stars that circle, or revolve around, each other.

calendar: a system for dividing time, most commonly into days, weeks, and months. Every calendar has a starting day and ending day for a year.

Caracol: an early observatory built by the Mayans in Chichén Itzá, Mexico.

comet: a small object in space made of ice, rock, and dust. When its orbit brings it closer to the Sun., it develops a tail of gas and dust. Early people often believed that comets predicted the occurrence of Earthly disasters.

constellation: a grouping of stars in the sky that seems to trace out a familiar pattern, figure, or symbol. Constellations are named after the shapes they resemble.

Dark Ages: a popular name for the early part of the Middle Ages. The Dark Ages covered a period of several hundred years that is often associated with a lack of learning throughout Europe.

eclipse: the total or partial blocking of light from one celestial body by another. During a solar eclipse, parts of Earth are in the shadow of the Moon as the Moon cuts across the Sun, which is thus briefly hidden from view in those areas. In a lunar eclipse, the Moon briefly passes through the shadow of Earth; during this time it is not lit by sunlight.

electromagnetic radiation: such forms of radiation as gamma rays, X rays, ultraviolet radiation, light, infrared radiation, radio waves, and microwaves.

light-year: the distance that light travels in one year — nearly six trillion miles (9.6 trillion kilometers).

nebula: a vast cloud of dust and gas in space.

observatory: a building or site designed for watching and recording celestial objects and events.

planet: a large celestial body that revolves around our Sun or some other star and that is not itself a star.

star map: a chart showing prominent stars and constellations.

sundial: an instrument to measure the time of day by the movement and location of the Sun.

supernova: the violent death of a large star in which most of its gas is blown into space in a huge explosion, which may be extremely bright.

telescope: an instrument used to observe distant objects. Telescopes that rely on light for observation are often made of lenses or mirrors

Tower of Babel: according to the Bible, a huge tower built by people who thought they could reach the heavens by climbing higher and higher into the sky.

Index

Born in 1920, Isaac Asimov came to the United States as a young boy from his native Russia. As a young man, he was a student of biochemistry. In time, he became one of the most productive writers the world has ever known. His books cover a spectrum of topics, including science, history, language theory, fantasy, and science fiction. His brilliant imagination gained him the respect and admiration of adults and children alike. Sadly, Isaac Asimov died shortly after the publication of the first edition of *Isaac Asimov's Library of the Universe*.

The publishers wish to thank the following for permission to reproduce copyright material: front cover, 3, © CORBIS; 4-5, 29 (upper left), © Garret Moore 1987; 6, © Frank Zullo; 7, © Kurt Burmann 1988; 8, Kunsthistorisches Museum; 9, 17 (both), 23 (upper), 29 (second row, center and right), © Mary Evans Picture Library; 10, Bishop Museum; 11, Courtesy of Moshe ben-Shimon; 12 (upper), 29 (second row, left), © Frank Reddy; 12 (lower), 22, 29 (upper right), 29, (third row, right), Science Photo Library; 13, United States Geological Survey; 14, 24 (large), Ann Ronan Picture Library; 15, 20 (large), 23 (lower), 27, The Granger Collection, New York; 16, Griffith Observatory; 18, Gérard Franquin/© Père Castor; 19, 26 (right), © Getty Images; 20 (inset), Collection Frederick R. Weisman Art Museum at the University of Minnesota, Minneapolis; 21, Adler Planetarium; 24 (inset), National Optical Astronomy Observatories; 25 (left), 29 (third row, left and center), Courtesy of Julian Baum; 25 (right), Paris Observatory; 26 (left), 29 (fourth row, center), Space Telescope Science Institute; 29 (fourth row, left), © Greg Vaughn/Tom Stack and Associates; 29 (fourth row, right), Courtesy of NRAO/AUI and ESO.Space Telescope Science Institute; 27, The Granger Collection, New York; 28 (upper), Science Photo Library; 28 (lower), 29 (upper left), © Garret Moore 1987; 29 (top center), Mary Evans Picture Library; 29 (upper right), © Frank Reddy; 29 (center left), Courtesy of Julian Baum; 29 (second from top, right), Mary Evans Picture Library; 29 (lower left), Science Photo Library; 29 (bottom center), © Greg Vaughn/Tom Stack and Associates; 29 (second from bottom, right), Courtesy of Julian Baum; 29 (lower right), Space Telescope Science Institute.